OUCH!

The record for playing the most innings with a wasp in the pants is one and one-half. It was set June 6, 1981, by third baseman Shawn Skinner of Wenatchee, Washington, two days before his eighth birthday.

At the bottom of the fifth inning, the first-grader began to squirm. He complained that a splinter was sticking him. His father checked, found nothing, and told him to play on. In the sixth inning, Shawn made all three putouts.

Back at the bench, Shawn opened his pants and away flew a yellow jacket. He had been stung twice in the leg and once in the rear.

His coach called him the best player he'd ever had, with or without a wasp.

Encyclopedia Brown's Third Record Book Of Weird And Wonderful Facts

By Donald J. Sobol

Illustrated by
Sal Murdocca

BANTAM BOOKS
TORONTO · NEW YORK · LONDON · SYDNEY · AUCKLAND

For Phyllis and Aress Solakian

RL 6, 008–012

ENCYCLOPEDIA BROWN'S THIRD RECORD BOOK
OF WEIRD AND WONDERFUL FACTS

A Bantam Skylark Book / November 1985

PRINTING HISTORY

William Morrow edition published September 1985

ISBN 0-553-15372-2

Published simultaneously in the United States and Canada

PRINTED IN THE UNITED STATES OF AMERICA

O   0 9 8 7 6 5 4 3 2 1

Acknowledgments

In preparing this book I received help from many sources. I wish especially to express my gratitude again to:

Agnes McFarlane of Montreal, Canada; Raymond J. Buck, Jr., of Storrs, Connecticut; Donald W. David of Destin, Florida; Jesse Davis, Paul Feehan, and Cecy and Richard Rowen of Miami, Florida; Russell E. Byerley of Port Richey, Florida; Rita Rogers of Zephyrhills, Florida; Olin J. Bates of Cedartown, Georgia; John Langford and Ben Tompkins of Rome, Georgia; Mrs. Ed L. Barrett of Stone Mountain, Georgia; Robert A. Delmotte of Georgetown, Illinois; Mrs. Leonard Culerson and Velma Kincaid of Burrton, Kansas; Alfred M. Collmann and Joy Moore of Haven, Kansas; Elmer Karstensen and Harold Wambsgans of Shawnee Mission, Kansas; Earl Powers and Edna "Tiny" Tarbutton of Baskin, Louisiana; Douglas Mazany of Saginaw, Michigan; James L. Toomey of St. Louis, Missouri; Dennis Wepman of New York City; Sandy Schwartz of Columbus, Ohio; David Creech of Franklin, Ohio; Steve Kick of Kenton, Ohio; Bill

Plummer III of Oklahoma City, Oklahoma; Dr. James A. Ruby of Oil City, Pennsylvania; Wayne McIntosh of Great Falls, South Carolina; Tom Kite of Austin, Texas; Homer E. Smith of Hutchins, Texas; Clifton Pitman of Pampa, Texas; Elizabeth McLaughlin of Middlebury, Vermont; Sandy Rinker of Mt. Jackson, Virginia; Judy Skinner of Wenatchee, Washington; Sister Mary DiDomenico of Fairmont, West Virginia.

And Rose, my wife, who without a murmur of complaint put up with two tons of newspapers and magazines every month.

—D.J.S.

Contents

Gender Gems

Circus performers who do strong-jaw acts are almost always women.

When sipping a drink, a man is more apt to peer into the glass or cup, a woman to look above the rim.

Women's vocal cords are shorter than men's, which is why their voices are higher. The shorter length also requires less air to agitate the cords, and so women can talk more with less effort.

Men are 3 times more likely than women to be the victims of violent crimes at the hands of strangers.

Rich men are usually fatter than rich women.

When examining her fingernails, a woman will usually extend her fingers palm down. A man will usually examine his nails by curling his fingers palm up.

Women usually enjoy vacations more.

When men and women chat with members of their own sex, women tend to sit much closer together.

Tests at Northwestern University show that men change their minds more frequently.

There are more variations among women's legs than among men's.

Nearly 85 percent of the people killed by lightning are male.

Women took over as telephone operators because tests showed that their voices were clearer than men's on the early telephones.

Water makes up about 60 percent of the average man's body weight, but only about 50 percent of the average woman's.

Men make better jurors than women. That's the verdict of a study by the University of Chicago Law School.

Women make better pearl divers than men.

Along with prettier smiles, women have cleaner ones. The American Dental Association says that three-fourths of adult women brush their teeth at least twice a day. Only half the adult men do.

Women enjoy meeting new people more than men do.

Although men are stronger overall, women are slightly stronger per pound of lean body weight.

Men have been noted to fall out of hospital beds twice as often as women.

Eye movements observed in a Harvard University study found that while watching a movie, women look at the heroine more than men do.

The average woman blows out a match; the average man shakes it out.

A woman at the peak of her strength (about the age of 25) has approximately the same muscle power as a 60-year-old man of the same size.

Men who snore outnumber women snorers 12 to 1.

Researchers have awakened to the fact that men have more pleasing dreams. Women's dreams tend to be disappointing and frustrating. Women also have more nightmares, but they remember their dreams better.

Men are better basketball shooters. One reason is that they are taller. The higher the ball is launched above the floor, the greater chance of its going through the hoop.

Music and the arts are largely patronized by women. Men go to the theater and to concerts on opening nights or on special nights to build their images. On such occasions, the audience is evenly divided between males and females. On most other nights, women outnumber men.

More boys than girls do household chores.

Women are more likely than men to live in poverty, according to the Census Bureau.

Nearly twice as many men as women have to be rescued by lifeguards.

More women than men travel on commercial airlines.

Stuttering occurs far more often in males.

Doctors take the complaints of women less seriously than those of men, and so examine female patients less thoroughly, a survey of doctors in La Jolla, California, suggests. One conclusion: doctors frequently think women are imagining their sickness.

A man has slightly more red corpuscles (which carry oxygen to the tissues) than a woman of the same size.

Color blindness affects 20 times as many men as women.

Women usually have a greater need to be hugged.

Men usually have a better sense of direction.

The ring finger is longer than the index finger on most men and shorter on most women.

Speeds up wedding ceremonies.

Far more girls than boys grow up knock-kneed.

Boys study better than girls in rooms where talking is going on, according to Dr. Daniel Christie, a psychologist at Ohio State University.

Background talk of normal level can actually help boys study better. The older the boys, the more they're helped.

Girls, who are more sensitive to language uses, need peace and quiet, Dr. Christie found. And the older the girls, the harder it is for them to concentrate in surroundings abuzz with conversation.

A woman needs less food than a man of equal weight, and so nearly 3 times as many women go on a diet to shed pounds. (Or maybe men lose weight more easily because they throw it around.)

Men sweat more than women, though this doesn't mean they have a better cooling system. Women sweat more efficiently—just enough. Men often sweat more than is necessary.

A woman skier tends to fall on her back, a man on his face. This has something to do with a woman's lower center of gravity. Sexist ski boots might help: hers with a raised heel, his with a raised toe.

Not skiing would help even more.

Teenage girls outspend teenage boys.

Stanford University scientists say that the genes that determine whether a person will have a lot or a little energy are passed down from the mother. Most other traits are inherited from either parent.

Women normally have more body fat than men of the same size. Stored in the thighs and buttocks, the fat gives them more buoyancy. This aids them in long-distance swimming.

When responding to the request, "Show me your hands," a man will usually hold out his hands palms up—a woman, palms down.

A University of Pennsylvania study found that the 10 leading female fears are, in order: fire, dead people, being rejected, mice or rats, failure, hurting the feelings of others, weapons, surgery, speaking in public, and looking down from tall buildings.

The 10 leading male fears are speaking in public, failure, hurting the feelings of others, looking foolish, falling, being rejected, surgery, being disapproved of, being criticized, and bats.

Women are more strongly opposed than men to defense spending and the death penalty. Similarly, they are more in favor of a lawful ban on handguns except for police and other authorized persons.

Males dream about females less often than about other males. Females dream about both sexes with equal frequency.

Most men who played on a varsity team in high school or college feel more healthy—and they *are*—than nonathletes. With women, the opposite is true—former high school or college athletes feel less healthy than nonathletes.

Male lefties outnumber female lefties 2 to 1.

Women suffer 4 times as many foot problems as men. Blame their shoes. High heels place almost all the weight on the ball of the foot and cramp the toes. Thinner soles, common in women's shoes, do not provide enough cushion.

During the Christmas shopping rush, sales clerks are more likely to serve men first and keep women waiting. In 1984, marketing tests were conducted at 21 Houston and Detroit department stores. Men were served first 63 percent of the time, regardless of whether the clerks were male or female.

Women are more scents-itive than men. Researchers at the University of Pennsylvania Medical School found that women smell better . . . er, that is, they smell better with their noses.

Gym Dandies

Travelin' man: Harvey Gartley, a 15-year-old boxer of Saginaw, Michigan, lost by a knockout in less than a minute without taking a punch. He didn't land one, either.

On January 31, 1977, Harvey, a novice bantamweight, fought Dennis Oulette of Rogers City in the 15th Annual Saginaw Regional Golden Gloves Tournament. At the bell, Harvey danced around the ring "to get myself into position to throw my first punch."

While his opponent missed with jabs and roundhouse swings, Harvey tripped the light fantastic. He danced himself into exhaustion, fell to the canvas, and was counted out after 47 seconds.

How did Harvey, who really wanted to be a baseball player, feel afterward?

"I'm happy and so are my parents," he said. "I didn't get hurt."

Awrrr: Watertown (New York) High School's football team had just scored a third-quarter touchdown against Amsterdam High on November 12, 1938. In the stands,

Rita McDonald, 17, a Watertown senior, opened her mouth to cheer—and couldn't get it shut.

"I wasn't frightened, just mystified," she said after spending a few hours in nearby Mercy Hospital, where her jaw was set. "My girlfriends thought I was trying to be funny."

Best dressed: A New York City clothing store owner offered a $25 gift certificate as first prize in a contest to pick the most winners in 80 football games in 1966. The winner: a Columbia University computer.

Never say die: No one ever won a basketball game single-handedly—till Pat McGee.

Pat accomplished the impossible in a game between the seniors and sophomores of St. Peter's School in Fairmont, West Virginia, on March 16, 1937. The score was tied, 32–32, when the last of Pat's senior teammates fouled out. Four minutes still remained.

Playing alone, Pat held the sophomores scoreless while he sank a field goal and a free throw for a 35–32 victory.

Bzzzt-dressed: The record for playing the most innings with a wasp in the pants is 1½. It was set on June 6, 1981, by third baseman Shawn Skinner of Wenatchee, Washington, 2 days before his eighth birthday.

At the bottom of the fifth inning, the first grader began to squirm. He complained that a sliver was sticking him. His father checked, found nothing, and told him to play on. In the sixth inning, Shawn made all 3 putouts.

Back at the bench, Shawn opened his pants and away flew a yellow jacket. He had been stung twice in the leg and once in the rear.

His coach called him the best player he'd ever had, with or without a wasp.

Kickback: In football, punts are supposed to advance the ball. On September 19, 1980, Craig Ward, kicker for Cortez (Colorado) High School, violated the notion and almost the law of gravity.

Ward's first punt against Aztec High was blocked. His second made a comeback: the ball went up in the air 25 yards and traveled 38 yards *backward*.

"I thought it was the world's best punt," he said. "But I didn't know where it went. Then I saw the whole Aztec team coming my way. I realized the ball was behind me."

Craig brought a 34-yard punting average into the game. His 4 punts that night worked out to a 2.5-yard average.

His team scored in the last quarter. But he missed the conversion, and the game ended in a 6–6 tie.

Feeling his outs: Bryant High School's baseball players didn't have to field a single hit—fair or foul—as they defeated Queens Vocational in New York City on April 29, 1982.

Bryant's pitcher, Clemente Alvear, 17, walked the first

batter, who was caught stealing. Clemente then struck out the next 20 batters in the 7-inning game.

Hit parade: Kenton hit on its first 15 shots from the floor while thumping Indian Lake, 99–55, in an Ohio high school basketball game on February 14, 1981.

A real charmer: Mary Hopf, 16, felt out of luck at the 1978 Junior Olympics in Lincoln, Nebraska. She had left

her box of lucky charms at home in McMurray, Pennsylvania.

Since her race was to be telecast, Mary called her sister long distance and had her set the box atop the TV set. The charms did their thing: Mary won the 1-mile walk.

Fast is fast; not short: The basketball game between East Boston High School and Chelsea High on January 24, 1906, was played in 15-minute halves.

The *Boston Globe* called it "probably the fastest game ever played."

Says who else? Definitely not the Chelsea players.

In those interminable 30 minutes, Chelsea made but one free throw. It wasn't enough to catch East Boston, who stuffed the basket at the rate of almost 5 points a minute and won, 149–1.

Power play: The two top-ranked Miami (Florida) high school football teams, Palmetto and Coral Gables, battled to a 0–0 tie on the night of September 11, 1978, in the Orange Bowl. The first overtime was halted in a way no one could have foreseen—or saw.

With the ball on its own 44-yard line, Coral Gables called a trick play. Quarterback Ed Angelo handed off to halfback Cyril Brown, who then tossed back to Ed. The ball was in the air when the power failed. The lights died, hiding the field in sudden darkness.

The next thing anyone knew, Ed was discovered in the end zone, waving the football. He had caught the pass, he claimed, and had sprinted through the darkness for a touchdown.

Coral Gables argued that the touchdown counted. Palmetto argued that some quick-thinker had shoved a football at Ed with the appeal to get going.

After 5 minutes the officials ruled it no touchdown. Meanwhile, the 5,800 fans began setting their programs afire to see what was happening. Nothing. After 15 minutes came the decision: the game was called, and the overtime would be replayed at another date.

Fifty-nine days later, Palmetto scored on its first play and won, 8–0.

At the 1908 Olympics in London, England, U.S. track star Forrest Smithson won the 110-meter hurdles while carrying a Bible in his hand for inspiration.

The men just weren't oriented: Basketball was first played in the Philippines by girls. In Japan, male athletes scorned the game until 1913, being convinced it was for the weaker sex only.

C. Alphonso Smith won national tennis titles 55 years apart. He captured the boys' singles championship in 1924. In 1978 he teamed with doubles partner Frank Goeltz to take the 70-and-over championship.

Hoop step: In a basketball game on December 19, 1980, Franklin and Lebanon, two Ohio high school teams, stayed as even with each other as a kangaroo's hind legs.

The score by quarters was 8–8, 22–22, 34–34, and 51–51. After a 3-minute overtime, the teams were still even, 53–53. Franklin won in the second overtime, 58–56.

How-to: Rip Collins, a first baseman with the Cardinals and Cubs, brought his work home. He used broken bats to build a fence around his house near Albany, New York.

That certain feeling: Bob Beamon of the U.S. long-jumped a fantastic 29 feet 2½ inches in winning the gold medal at the 1968 Olympics. A computer analysis of the leap showed his hip joint generated 1,700 pounds of force. That's enough to wreck the muscles of an ordinary man.

That uncertain feeling: Guy Gertsch, 38, of Salt Lake City, Utah, ran most of the 1982 Boston Marathon with a broken thighbone.

At the seventh mile he felt what he thought was a cramp. The pain worsened, but he kept going. His powerfully developed thigh muscles acted as a splint that held the broken bone together. He collapsed at the finish, having clocked an amazing 2 hours and 47 minutes.

Basketball coach Jim Lankster expressed his low opinion of an opponent that had defeated his St. Camillus Academy team of Corbin, Kentucky, by a measly 21 points in 1973.

"This is the worst team we've ever played," stated Lankster flatly. "It's nothing for us to get beat by one hundred points."

On the rebound: On February 20, 1972, Venango Christian High School of Oil City, Pennsylvania, did everything but steal the backboards in running over East

Forest High, 104–62. Venango set a national high school basketball l-game record for rebounding—121.

Star of the day was Venango's Mark Garbacz, 17, but not because he led all the scorers with 37 points. The 6-foot-4-inch, 215-pound junior established an individual record with 55 rebounds, even though he played only 3 quarters.

Now that's service for you: No one in America has ever served a volleyball better than Sandy Rinker, 15, of the Stonewall Jackson (Virginia) High School girls team.

During a span of the 1980–81 season, the blue-eyed 5-foot-7½-inch sophomore was perfection. In 6 matches (13 games), she cannonballed her left-handed serve 109 straight times without a fault, helping her team to the regional title. Against runner-up Page High, she served 25 consecutive points—all 15 of one game and 10 of the next. (She had served every point in two other games earlier that season.) Almost routinely she banged aces, balls that opponents could not return.

The Philadelphia Eagles gained less than 1 yard per rushing play for the entire 1940 season.

The good earth: Troy Roberts, 17, of Chester (South Carolina) High School dreamed up an idea to promote interest in the football team.

The 6-foot, 198-pound senior offensive tackle promised to eat 1 earthworm for every point Chester outscored its opponents in 1980.

The team ended the season at 5 and 5. Altogether, Troy ate 90 worms, including a 41-wormer after a 48-7 bash of York High. He downed the worms raw and said they tasted like noodles dipped in sand.

He suffered no ill effects. Nonetheless, the next year,

when he went to college, he chose Winthrop, which hasn't got a football team.

Albert Von Tilzer, who composed "Take Me Out to the Ball Game" in 1908, had never seen a baseball game and couldn't have cared less about the sport.

The longest streak: A record to shoot at belongs to the girls of tiny Baskin (Louisiana) High School. The Lady

Rams won more basketball games in a row than any team (boys' or girls') in history—218.

This hard-to-believe streak began with a 50–15 rout of Ogden High on November 11, 1947, stretched across 7 years, and included the first 5 of 7 straight Class B State Championships. There were only Class A and Class B schools in Louisiana then. Baskin, a rural school with 450 students in grades 1 through 12, played against any school within 30 miles, regardless of size. They also played in invitational tournaments. To support the team, the players held raffles and cake walks.

The girls stressed teamwork under Coach Edna

Tarbutton and had few individual stars. It took a much larger, Class A school, Winnsboro, to snap the 218-game streak on January 5, 1953. The score was 37–33.

After the loss, Baskin bounced back and won 71 games before another defeat.

When the gang's all here: Place kicking is a science. The snap, the hold, the turf, and the wind all have to be right.

After kicking 5 field goals against Green Bay before a packed house in 1980, Detroit's Eddie Murray added another factor—the crowd.

"The air is dead when the stadium is empty," Murray confided. "When there are more people, the ball carries. It just flies off my foot."

Twenty-four years after Roger Bannister ran the first under-4-minute mile (3:59.4), Antti Loikkanen of Finland clocked 3:54.38 in a race in West Germany. Loikkanen finished *thirteenth*. On the same day, August 8, 1980, 12 other milers broke 4 minutes in a meet in London.

Tossin' and turnin': Clifton Anthony "Cap" Pitman, 12, of Pampa, Texas, introduced a whirlaround pitching motion in 1980 that threw Little League officials from coast to coast into a dizzy tizzy.

A first baseman, Cap was pressed into service as a pitcher on June 12. The team's regular hurler had broken a toe; the reliever had come down with chicken pox.

Cap was ready. The 4-foot-9-inch right-hander had honed his unique delivery by tossing a tennis ball during a neighborhood pickup game. The whirling motion enabled him to throw harder even if it tired his arm sooner.

In action, he began by facing first base. He pumped his arms once and pivoted. As he spun, his left leg pointed at first base, then at second, and finally, at third, while his right foot held the mound. Then he extended and *zoom*— the ball slammed into the catcher's mitt.

Opposing players got on him. They called him "Ballerina," and their fans took up the ribbing. Rival coaches rushed onto the field screaming, "Balk!" Motion pictures of his turnstile pitch were sent to Little League headquarters for judgment. The ruling came back. The delivery was legal.

By then the season was over. Cap had compiled a 2 and 0 record (plus one no-decision). Few batters had hit him. As his coach put it, "He either walked 'em or struck 'em out."

Some 5,000 TV viewers had their day in Columbus, Ohio, on July 12, 1980. By means of hookups with a central computer, they called the plays for the local football team, the Columbus Metros.

The Monday-morning quarterbacks got sacked. The Metros lost to the Racine Gladiators, 10–7.

Great Scott!: Steve Scott of the U.S. ran the world's fastest unofficial mile—3:31.25—on April 3, 1982. His time slashed a whopping 16.08 seconds off the world record of 3:47.33 held by Sebastian Coe of England.

How did Scott do it? Not with rockets. The course was the main street of Auckland, New Zealand. Straight and downhill all the way.

Walk, don't run, to the nearest base: In its first varsity baseball game, Princeton Christian School couldn't get a hit off 3 pitchers from Island Christian School on March 12, 1981, in Islamorada, Florida. Princeton did get 21 walks, enough to stroll around the bases for a 12–4 win.

Make way for courage: Ed L. Barrett scored 32 touchdowns to lead his Cedartown (Georgia) High School football team to an undefeated season in 1928. The following August he lost his left arm below the elbow in a hunting accident. Forced to miss the 1929 season, he stayed close to football by reporting the school's games for the local newspaper.

In 1930 he returned to action as team captain. On the field the 5-foot-9-inch, 130-pound right halfback wore a leather shield cushioned with a sponge. He used the shield to deliver jolting stiff-arms.

It was as a pass catcher, not as a runner, however, that he gave his most extraordinary performance. On October 31, 1930, as Cedartown defeated Rome High, one-handed Ed Barrett caught 4 passes and intercepted 3.

Small wonder: Gene Mirkin, 8, of Rockville, Maryland, ran a mile in 5:40 in 1971. Overnight he became a sensation.

At the age of 11, Gene quit competitive running, though his family had hoped to train him for the 1980 Olympics.

Years later, as an 18-year-old college freshman, Gene looked back upon his headline days as a running whiz.

"I just wanted to be a kid," he said.

For good luck, Mark Van Eeghen, an NFL running back for the Raiders, dived off his television set into bed the night before each game.

If you field a baseball like a magnet but wonder why you're hitting .222, consider what you're up against.

A fastball traveling at 90 mph arrives at the plate in less than ½ a second. So the batter has only ¼ of a second to make up his mind whether to swing. Then he has about another ¼ of a second to bring the bat above the plate, which the ball crosses in about ¹/₁₀₀ of a second.

It's all in the timing: The 3 leaders in the women's 53-kilometer (33 miles) race at the 1981 World Cycling Championships in Prague, Czechoslovakia, stuck closer together than bark on a tree.

Ute Enzenauer, 16, of West Germany, nipped Jennie Longo of France and Connie Carpenter of the U.S. to win. All 3 were timed in 1:30.2—and so were the next 5 finishers!

Matthew Garrett, 6, of Solana Beach, California, was a one-boy gang on the soccer field in 1981. He scored 83

goals to lead the Firecrackers of the Solana youth league to a 12 and 0 record and the division title. In one game he had 14 goals.

A as in apple: At Pittsburgh Air Force Base, members of the 1980 U.S. winter Olympic team were greeted by well-wishers. The line of autograph-seekers was moving nicely till it hit a bottleneck. A rugged individual, age 6, demanded that the athletes *print* their names.

On borrowed time: Two Shawnee Mission (Kansas) high school football teams, South and West, were battling in a Class 6A playoff game on November 20, 1981. Four seconds were left—time for one play.

South held a 24–21 lead, the ball, and a certain victory. South's quarterback, Butch Ross, had only to take the final snap and, as a spectator shouted ungrammatically, "lay down."

But it's a long, long way from lay to remember, and Butch forgot.

Instead of grounding the ball, he raised it aloft and jubilantly trotted toward his own goal as the 4 seconds ran out.

South fans poured onto the field. Butch was preparing to shake hands with a cousin when West's quarterback-safety, John Reichart, heeded the screams from his bench: "He never downed it! He never downed it!"

The play wasn't dead. And neither was the game. The 4 officials waited. . . .

John ran up behind Butch, snatched the ball, and raced 40 yards for a touchdown and a West victory, 27–24.

Really battered: Infielder Ron Hunt covered himself with bruises as well as records during his National League career from 1963 to 1974. He was hit by 243 pitched balls. For 7 consecutive seasons he led the league as the batter most often hit by pitchers.

Nobody said it was easy: The final score was 56–39. The sport? No, not basketball. Women's softball.

The University of Connecticut at Stamford, playing its

first intercollegiate softball game, outlasted Mohegan Community College. The 6-inning contest, called on account of darkness, lasted 4 hours and 40 minutes. In addition to 95 runs, the game produced 48 hits, 50 walks, and 17 errors.

The defeat dropped the losers' record to 0 and 2 for the season. Still, coming up only 17 runs short represented an improvement. In its opener, Mohegan had been beaten by 34 runs, 35–1.

In 1979 Italian customs agents seized a boa constrictor named Pedro that an American fighter wore into the ring to unnerve opponents.

Hot shot: When Cheryl Miller, 18, of Riverside, California, was named to the 1982 *Parade* magazine All-America girls' basketball team, she became the only player ever selected to the first team 4 times. The 6-foot-2-inch, 145-pound ace racked up a 37.70-point average, with a single game high of 105.

Against Norte Vista High on January 29, 1981, Cheryl outdid the world. She became the first female to score on a dunk in a regulation contest. Moreover, she did it the hard way, slamming home a *two-hander,* as her team, Riverside Poly, won, 137–11.

Cheryl went on to lead the United States women's basketball team to a gold medal in the 1984 Olympics in Los Angeles.

Hottest shot: While suiting up for a Canadian junior ice hockey game on February 16, 1930, schoolboy Abie Goldberry moved some articles from his trousers to the back pocket of his hockey shorts. Included were a book of matches and a Celluloid comb.

Abie, a goalie for Dufferin Square, was getting along fine until the second period. Then the puck from a hard shot struck his back pocket, and the friction from the blow ignited the matches, which exploded the Celluloid comb, which set fire to his pants.

He was rushed to the hospital, and without him, his team lost, 2–0.

Known for his honestee: Pro golfer Tom Kite, 29, of Austin, Texas, was lining up his putt on the fifth green of the 1978 Hall of Fame Golf Tournament. He grounded his putter behind the ball, causing the ball to roll slightly. Although no one else saw the ball move, Kite penalized himself a stroke. The stroke eventually cost him a chance for a first-place playoff and $34,000 in prize money.

Dare to be dull: A staring match between a pair of snails is a carnival of thrills compared to the basketball game played by two Illinois high schools on March 6, 1930.

Georgetown upset heavily favored Homer by the score of 1–0.

Coach Don Sweely told his Georgetown squad not to take any shots if they got ahead. Anyone who dared would come out of the game and stay out. It was their only chance to win.

His players believed him.

Georgetown forward Clarence Stasavich sank a free throw in the first minute. The team then went into the longest stall since the Hundred Years' War.

The Georgetown guards, Baldwin and Parks, sat on the floor at their end of the court and tossed the ball back and forth. To break the monotony, they stood up and tossed the ball back and forth. Their teammates, meanwhile, chatted with the Homer players and the crowd.

Near the end of the sleepytime special, the regular sign, "Three Minutes to Play," was changed to "Three Minutes to Wait." At that point, Homer realized that though they were only 1 point behind, they could lose.

By then it was too late.

Up, up, and in: As a 16-year-old junior at Wilmer-Hutchins High School in Hutchins, Texas, Anthony "Spud" Webb played junior varsity basketball. He stood 4 feet 11 inches. During the summer of 1980 he grew 5 inches, filled out to 105 pounds, and literally jumped his way onto the varsity team.

A point guard and team leader, he was named All-Metro, All-District, All-State, All-Regional, and, twice, All-Tournament. He wasn't especially fast, but, oh, could he *jump*!

Against Dunbar High of Fort Worth, he took a pass in midcourt, drove to the basket, soared, arched his back, and . . . brought down the house.

Anthony, all 5 feet 4 inches of him, had done what he'd trained himself to do in practice—slam a one-handed dunk!

One Lioners
and Bushy Tales

Oinks fair in love and war: A pig on San Juan Island, Washington, brought the United States and Great Britain to the brink of war in the mid-1880s.

An American, Lyman Cutler, shot a pig belonging to a British magistrate, Charles Griffin. Both sides sent troops to the island. The dispute, known as the Pig War, was settled by an international body. It awarded the island to the United States.

In 1980 game wardens in Tabola National Park, India, posted signs by a lake filled with crocodiles. The signs read: "Swimming is forbidden. Survivors will be arrested."

Most bears are left-handed. A bear in the wild will almost always throw its weight on the right paw and work with the left.

To match the acceleration of a striking rattlesnake's head, you'd have to drive a car from zero to 60 mph in ½ a second.

Don't blame the stork: Research hints at a new explanation for the extinction of the dinosaur: too many babies were born of the same sex.

Experiments with the dinosaur's distant cousin, the

alligator, have shown the influence of temperature in determining the sex of offspring. If the temperature is at or below 30 degrees centigrade, the alligator babies will be born female. At or above 34 degrees centigrade, the babies will be male.

A sudden change in climate 65 million years ago—cooling or warming—may have caused the dinosaur to produce too many offspring of one sex. So, eventually, the huge beasts were unable to reproduce at all.

Not for rent: If you want your racing pigeon to fly faster, heed the advice of Eddie Abramoski of Buffalo, New York.

"Stick another male bird in your bird's nest," counsels Abramoski. "Your bird gets excited and races home that much faster because he doesn't want another bird taking over."

Samuel D. Riddle, who died in 1963, left nearly $4 million in his will to maintain the grave of his racehorse, Man o' War.

This is off the wall: Mike Turri, staff artist at the Memphis Zoo, decorated the zoo's buildings with lifelike scenes of Africa and South America. His painting on the wall of the birdhouse turned out to be *too* lifelike.

Finches started to fly into the wild blue yonder and

smacked into concrete. After a flock of headaches, the finches finally realized what had gone on.

The lowly caterpillar has more muscles than you have—better than 4,000 against your 639.

So how come they don't enter Mr. America contests?

Say it with flowers: The male euglossa bee mops up the liquid scent from orchids with its foreleg hairs, squeezes the juice into slits in its hind legs, alters the scent within itself, and spews the result through its head to attract females.

Let's have a smelling bee!

Recipe for egg drop soup: Sea gulls used oyster shells to bombard cars parked in a new lot in Cambridge, Maryland, in 1981. The parking lot had been built where the birds liked to nest.

Let sleeping dogs lie: Joggers who take their dogs along on a 6-mile run should be more considerate.

Canine joggers with bad knees, blistered footpads, strained ligaments, and even hip trouble are turning up at veterinary hospitals.

"Dogs are like people," said a veterinarian. "They have to be worked up to jogging. A dog will run until he drops if that is what his owner wants him to do."

That's the way the fruit flies: In 1978 memory researchers at Princeton University successfully bred an amnesic fruit fly, which forgets odors 4 times as fast as a normal fruit fly.

Rooster booster: Julie Koral, 14, of Rogue River, Oregon, understood about cock-a-doodle-doos. For 2 weeks she kept her pet rooster, Crow-In Joe, in a covered cage and far away from the cackle of hens.

She let him out at the 1981 Rogue River National Rooster Crow competition. Crow-In Joe was so pent-up that he crowed like crazy—82 times in 30 minutes—and won. His fast-paced fanfare defeated dozens of roosters from several states and earned Julie 150 silver dollars.

Scientists suspect that when a whale sleeps only half of its brain sleeps. The other half stays alert for danger.

Meanwhale. . . .

The crow is probably the smartest of all birds.

Hog heaven: William Pace, a farmer from Rienzi, Mississippi, doesn't let his hogs wallow around in the mud and heat. He fattens them in the milk barn under a giant fan and lets them watch TV.

Pace got the idea from dairies, which play the radio for Bossy's benefit. He reasoned that if cows like radio, hogs would love television.

And what is the hogs' favorite program?

"Wrestling," Pace said. "I know that's hard to believe, but I'm sure of it."

For goodness' quakes: A few months before a huge earthquake smote China in 1974, ordinary animals began acting strangely.

Hens didn't roost. Pigs climbed walls and nipped each other's tails. Hibernating snakes slithered out of the ground. Barnyard geese wouldn't fly. Trained German shepherds refused commands.

The Chinese heeded the animals' behavior. Several hundred thousand lives were saved when the region was evacuated 2 days before the quake struck.

It is estimated that between 1650 and 1850, a species of bird or mammal died out about once every 5 years. Between 1900 and 1950, 1 species disappeared every 8 months. Today, the rate is about 1 species per day.

The same degree of overweight is commonly found in older dogs and their masters. Cats are different; they're not inclined to eat to please their owners.

In the money with the tooth fairy: Lucy, 41, an Asian elephant at the San Diego Zoo, lost nearly 700 pounds in 1981. A sore tooth prevented her from chewing food.

After putting her to sleep with enough drugs—well, to knock out an elephant—a dentist removed the 5-pound molar with an electric drill, a crowbar, and a sledgehammer.

And ruined her smile.

The olyapka is a water sparrow that lives in Russia and feeds at the *bottom* of mountain springs. Its wings serve as fins as it swims underwater.

The country's only monument to a chicken is the pointed granite stone on the village common in Adamsville, Rhode Island. It marks the place where the famous breed the Rhode Island Red originated.

His lips are sealed: The harp seal is a mammal that has been stringing scientists along for years. They can't figure out how, with lungs no larger than a human's, it can dive *at least* 600 feet and stay underwater for about ½ an hour.

Scratch if it itches: Dead, 36 mosquitoes cover 1 square inch. Alive, 2 mosquitoes, free of enemies, could produce enough offspring in 1 season to cover the earth with a layer of mosquitoes more than a foot deep.

The loudest snorers in the animal kingdom are elephants, camels, sheep, cows, dogs, cats, gorillas, chimps, buffalo, and zebras.

Roll over, Dumbo.

The manatee is harmless, friendly, and defenseless. It dwells in warm Florida waters, looks like a bloated seal, and is gentle as a cushion. Although it can grow up to 12 feet in

length and weigh 1 ton, it will not fight, even to protect itself or save its young.

Some spiders are balloonists. First they climb to the top of a stalk or post. Then they shoot out several strands of silk, which the breeze catches, yanking them aloft. A spider may soar ½ a mile above the ground and land hundreds of miles away.

An anteater, which can flick its tongue 160 times a minute, eats up to 30,000 ants a day.

Sing along: Miners during the nineteenth century carried canaries down into the shafts with them. If his bird stopped singing, a miner knew the air was about to give out.

The buck stopped here: A male deer wrecked about $2,000 worth of merchandise in a sporting goods store in Cockeysville, Maryland, in 1980. It entered the store by smashing its way through a window that displayed hunting licenses.

All hopped up: To walk, the kangaroo uses its tail as a lever to raise its hind legs off the ground and allow them to swing forward. That's heavy work. Walking at only 3 mph, the kangaroo burns 4 times as much energy as a four-legged creature of the same size.

But hopping is something else. Then the kangaroo becomes graceful and efficient. To go faster, it doesn't take more hops, just longer ones, as it zips from food patch to food patch. Once it shifts from walking to hopping, it needs less oxygen. In tripling its speed from 7 mph to 21 mph, its oxygen use drops 5 to 10 percent. A four-legged animal of equal size increases its oxygen use by 150 percent to achieve similar increases in speed.

This thrifty fuel system, scientists believe, permitted the

kangaroo to survive while other grass-eaters died out. Hopping to the brief, widely spaced grassy spots of the Australian desert, the kangaroo didn't use up more energy getting to food than the food gave it.

Quit hounding me: Despite what you see in the movies, criminals can't escape bloodhounds by wading in streams or swimming across rivers. The scent lingers above the water, and the bloodhounds can follow it.

Pemaquid was 1 of 10 seals that frolicked at the New England Aquarium, and the only one that seemed to like swallowing coins. He caught the coins, thrown by visitors, in midair or scooped them off the bottom of the pool.

After a few months of showing off, Pemaquid began acting penny-pinched and nickel nutty. He underwent a 2-hour operation at Boston Hospital in 1980. When it was all over, surgeons had removed 278 coins, and Pemaquid was lighter by $8.97.

If angered enough, a 40-pound chimp can beat up a wrestler.

You can put a chicken to sleep all by yourself. Lay it on the ground and tuck its head under its wing for a count of about 100. It will snooze for a couple of minutes.

The dung beetle eats night and day for 2 months without stopping for a second.

Not even a burp.

Every dog has its day: The title "best looking pair of legs" at the University of Washington in 1981 belonged to the school's mascot pooch, Denali.

The 5-month-old malamute faced some tough, two-legged competition from 9 male and female human contestants. But the students, who raised $411 for the United Way, picked the furry foursome. The runner-up was Diane Eng, a cheerleader.

Baa baa blue sheep: In 1981 the U.S. Navy commissioned 50 goats to help cut the grass at the Oceana Naval Air Station in Virginia Beach, Virginia.

The goats nibbled the grassy outsides of ammunition bunkers, relieving the two-legged sailors for more important duties and saving the Navy about $20,000 yearly.

Raymond Long, a veterinary surgeon of London, England, started the first blood bank for dogs in 1972.

And it drew great interest.

Charge, kitty, charge: A Chinese firm in 1982 marketed an "electric cat" that zapped mice with an electric charge. A flashing red light, accompanied by the "meow-meow" of a cat, announced the kill. The gadget sold for $35.80.

When hunting, a polar bear will sometimes cover its black nose with a paw in order to blend completely into the surrounding white ice.

Who gives a hoot: The wise old owl is no brain trust. Even geese are far smarter. No matter. Owls are still good for catching roaches.

The national sport on Nauru, a tiny Pacific island, is lassoing birds in flight.

How heavenly: The starfish feeds by shoving its stomach through its mouth, covering its prey, and digesting the food outside its body.

In Bogotá, Colombia, in 1981, the Treasury Department had trouble with its files—rats kept eating them.

Since there wasn't enough money to buy rat poison, authorities appealed to the citizenship to donate cats for the war on the file-filching rodents.

Rat's nice.

Mongooses, those small animals that can kill cobras, were introduced into Hawaii in 1893. Sugar planters imported them to hunt rats.

After the mongooses arrived and multiplied, a blunder came to light. The mongoose roams by day, the rat by night. In Hawaii today, mongooses are considered pests nearly as bad as rats.

Come and Get It

Michael "Eat-All" Lotito of France broke his own record by eating 15 pounds of bicycle in 1979. The best part, he said, was the chain.

The Japanese consider the fugu, a blowfish, among the rarest and tastiest of foods. Yet specially licensed chefs must first remove the poisonous parts, which are many times more deadly than the poison strychnine.

Jesse James, the western outlaw, once refused to rob a bank in McKinney, Texas, because his favorite chili parlor was in the town.

In a 6-pack, the containers cost more to produce than the beverage.

If you've had a bowl of clam chowder lately, the chances are you ate a clam more than 100 years old. And maybe one 150 years old.

Two Purdue University psychologists discovered that on Halloween, kids wearing masks are twice as likely to sneak extra goodies from the offering as barefaced kids.

The Romans disliked the taste of swordfish and prayed to Neptune to keep it away from their nets.

King Charles XII of Sweden buttered his bread with his thumb.

Persons dining alone tip waiters 5½ percent more than do groups of 4 to 6.

In bygone days, the feast at a Bedouin wedding was a marvel of stuffing. To start, a fish was stuffed with eggs. The fish was then baked inside a chicken. The chicken became the stuffing of a whole sheep, which was roasted on a spit. The roasted sheep was sewn inside a camel, which was baked in a specially built oven.

The world's first-known fishing rod was dug up with the remains of a man who died 10,000 years ago in northern France.

Peanuts are used in the manufacture of ink dyes, shaving cream, paper, shoe polish, and floor cleaners.

Yüan Mei, a Chinese philosopher, was a chef with a delicate touch. He cooked his rice in dew that he gathered at dawn.

After astronauts Virgil "Gus" Grissom and John Young had made a triple orbital flight on March 31, 1965, officials were surprised to find one of the dehydrated, packaged meals uneaten.

Young had chosen to lunch on a bologna sandwich that he had smuggled aboard.

Orange juice is the most popular fruit juice in the U.S., and prune juice is the least popular. But the most popular canned juice is tomato, with grapefruit second, apple third, and orange fourth.

Percy Bysshe Shelley, the English poet, worked his brain harder than his stomach. Upon leaving his study, he frequently had to ask his wife, "Mary, have I dined?"

The shopping list of the National Zoo in Washington, D.C., includes some strange groceries. To keep the more finicky eaters happy, the zoo each year buys 96,000 rats and mice, 114,000 crickets, and 180,000 maggots.

Scientists in Manila, Philippines, say that termites are nutritious and delicious if served with hamburgers and omelets.

The Tridacna gigas is a giant clam found in the Pacific and Indian oceans. It is as big as 4 feet in width and weighs up to 200 pounds.

If you meet one, eat it before it eats you.

Growing enough wheat for a 1-pound loaf of bread requires 2 tons of water.

In 1979 gold miners in Alaska discovered the fully preserved carcass of an ancestor of the buffalo. It had walked the earth more than 20,000 years ago. Dale Guthrie, a scientist, nibbled the flesh and pronounced it good.

The animal was stored in the deep freeze at the University of Alaska. For the laboratory, not the cafeteria.

If you want to lose weight, color your kitchen green or blue, says Betsy Gabb of the University of Nebraska. Both colors are calming and discourage hunger pangs.

"Fast-food places," she says, "are done in hot orange and red to stimulate appetite and move out customers quickly."

Sir Isaac Newton, the famous English scientist, once had a joke played on him at a dinner party. A friend slipped some chicken bones onto his empty plate. Newton, who could never remember if he'd eaten, assumed that he had downed the meal and didn't ask for more.

Philip Ydzik of Olyphant, Pennsylvania, visited Chicago in 1955 and was so aroused by the sights that he ate 77 hamburgers at a single sitting. He washed the feast down with 6 quarts of milk and 6 soft drinks.

Alphonso, King of Castile, hated the odor of garlic so much that in 1368 he passed a law to protect himself. No knight who had eaten garlic could appear before him for at least a month.

If you drink tea from a polystyrene foam cup, don't add lemon. The cup might dissolve.

Among the earliest chocolate fanciers were the Aztecs of Mexico. They added hot peppers and spices to flavor it.

Tomoyuki Ono of Tokyo, Japan, developed a squarish watermelon approximately 7 inches by 7 inches by 7 inches.

In 1979, two of Tokyo's largest department stores sold them for $19.95 apiece. At the time, the average U.S. supermarket watermelon, the kind that just lies there waiting to be eaten, sold for about $5.00.

Said Ono, a designer: "My main object is to market them as art."

British scientists have developed a fly-catching potato. The purpose is to wipe out plagues of greenflies and other insects that ruin potato crops.

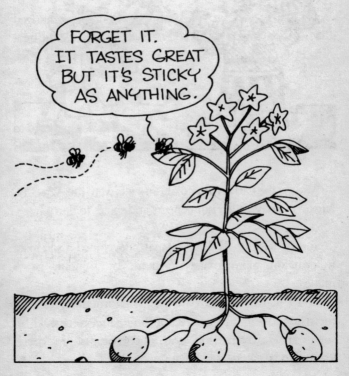

The new potato plant's leaves have millions of tiny hairs, which contain sticky gum. The greenflies become entangled and die of exhaustion and starvation before they can breed or harm the plant.

Ice cream originated in China. The diary of the fourteenth-century Italian traveler Marco Polo tells of "dishes of ice . . . flavored with exotic fruit."

His Italian companions liked it so much they changed the name to "Italian ices." Later the French turned the treat into its present form by adding cream and naming it ice cream.

Ezra Dagget invented the can in 1819. It was first used to preserve oysters, lobsters, and salmon.

How do you tell a vegetable from a fruit? The U.S. Supreme Court in 1893 ruled, in effect, that a plant most commonly eaten as part of the main course of a meal is a vegetable. One eaten as an appetizer, dessert, or between meals is a fruit.

Russians have never heard of Russian dressing. Danish pastry is called Vienna cakes in Denmark. Spanish rice is unknown in Spain.

Catis, a queen of ancient Syria, was wildly fond of fish. In order to ensure herself of the choicest supply, she ordered all fish caught within her kingdom to be brought before her.

Jay Schneider, 11, of Atlanta, Georgia, lost more than a title in his chess match against Mike Deck, 29, in 1979. He lost his appetite.

At stake was the World Chocolate Chess Championship. The pieces were made of chocolate, and the rules required the players to eat each captured piece.

A local television station tried to film the match. The crew, however, arrived late and had trouble convincing Jay to eat another piece.

Never on Sunday: The ice-cream soda was introduced by Robert M. Green at the Franklin Institute Exposition in Philadelphia, Pennsylvania, in 1874. The sparkling drink was an overnight sensation, except with some clergymen. In Newport, Vermont, in 1890, a sermon warned against the sin of "sucking soda" on Sunday. A little later, Evanston, Illinois, became the first city to pass a law against the "Sunday Soda Menace."

Finders Keepers?

That's a lot-tery of money: Joan Campaign of Adelaide, Australia, found a wallet with $225 in it in 1978. Although tempted to pocket the money, she handed it over to the police.

The grateful owner sent Campaign a reward—a 55-cent lottery ticket. The next week the ticket won her a car, a boat and trailer, and a mobile home—worth $45,000 in all.

One for the books: For a little while a New York City mailman walked around like an oil baron.

Harold Norris, 45, withdrew some money from his savings account at the Chase Manhattan Bank in 1981. Later he glanced at his savings book and his eyeballs skittered.

"I looked at the page and said, 'Wait a minute! What the heck is the 9 doing there with all those commas after it?'" he recalled.

Following the withdrawal, his bank balance should have

read $4,524.35. A computer flub listed the balance as a sky-high $9,904,524.35!

Norris returned to the bank to correct the error, but not right away. He talked with friends and enjoyed the sensation of being a multimillionaire.

"A buddy," he said, "told me to take out the eight million and leave the rest in the bank—and get on a fast boat."

Could he have kept the $9.9 million overpay?

"No way," declared a bank spokesman. "Nothing went into his account. It was just on the book."

Still, not everyone has a day like that to remember.

Follow that Frisbee!: Tom Golik, 11, was tossing a Frisbee with his friend John Humphreys in a field near their homes in Coral Gables, Florida, in 1981. A bad toss started the boys searching through some thick underbrush.

Instead of the missing Frisbee, Tom found a half-open box of jewels—$1,200 worth.

Police identified the jewels as part of $12,000 in diamonds, bracelets, and gold chains burgled from 3 apartments in the same building within a 2-day period.

One of the victims, Ann Williamson, got back some of the jewelry stolen from her. She gave Tom $20.

"I had to do something for him," Williamson said. "There are not that many honest folks around. He restored my faith in people."

"I hope they catch the crooks," said Tom. "I want to be a policeman, just like the ones who took the reports."

With a lootle bit of luck: In 1976 the back doors of a Purolator company van flew open in Philadelphia, Pennsylvania, and out tumbled $54,000. Motorists scooped up the money. Purolator officials blamed "a bad bounce on the highway."

Five years later the back doors of another Purolator van flew open, in Philadelphia once again. This time $1.2 million tumbled to the pavement. Brakes squealed, but not the van's. Out jumped a passenger from a car behind. He snatched up the loot and became an instant millionaire.

Easy come, easy go: Nine fourth-graders in Stillwater, Oklahoma, sat down in a circle to talk things over in 1982. They had just stumbled upon a wallet with $350 in it.

Those who advanced the "finders keepers" argument

were outnumbered. The vote went in favor of "honesty is the best policy."

The owner of the wallet, Steve Freeman, was so pleased to get his wallet back that he gave the children $20. A second vote was taken. The decision was to spend the money immediately—at the movies.

Down in the dumps: In 1979, a restaurant owner in Palm Springs, California, fearing a robbery, put $20,000 in a cardboard box and hid it in a trash bin for safekeeping.

Her caution backfired. The next morning was trash pickup day, and hers went to the local dump. The frantic woman rushed to trash headquarters with her tale of woe. Officials called out everyone but the Texas Rangers to sift through tons of trash from all over Coachella Valley.

Garbageman Ruben Nieto, 24, joined the search. He kicked over the box, spilling out the $20,000.

Nieto learned that virtue sometimes has to be its own reward. The restaurant owner gave him a $20 bill.

When all is said and Dunn: In 1982, Charles Dunn of Lee's Summit, Missouri, was taken aback when he discovered $5,500 inside a toolbox he had bought for $15. And so was the 64-year-old woman who sold it to him.

Dunn had made his purchase at a garage sale the week before. He kept the toolbox, but returned the money to the woman.

"When I gave it to her, she was halfway between laughing and crying," he said. "She couldn't even count it she was so nervous."

The toolbox had belonged to the woman's husband, who had died 4 years earlier.

Dunn, 37, said his family goes to garage sales and swap meets because "we don't have the money to buy all the things we need."

The first thought that ran through his mind was that the money was legally but not morally his.

"It's a good lesson to my son," Dunn said. "If parents can't be honest, how can they expect their children to be honest?"

Cashing in her chips: Ginger Stewart, 21, of Indianapolis, Indiana, bought a bag of potato chips in 1981 and got more than she paid for. Inside the bag, along with the crunchy snack, was a wallet containing $27, credit cards, and identification.

The wallet belonged to Thomas Kelley, 26, of Terre Haute, a mechanic at the company that made the potato chips. About 3 weeks earlier, the wallet had fallen out of his pocket, glanced off something, and bounced onto the conveyor belt.

"I never expected to see it again," Kelley said. "I thought

a fellow in a bar somewhere might open a bag of chips one day and get a surprise."

Said Stewart, "It was weird—not your everyday occurrence."

Windfall city: Walking past a store in Chicago, Illinois, in 1981, David Hermiz, 16, and Charles Marcol, 18, saw a briefcase by the front door. The boys couldn't resist a peek.

The peek revealed $7,000 in cash, $3,400 in checks, and the keys to the store and its alarm system.

The boys took the briefcase to David's house and told the police. Yashbant Shah, the store's owner, and his nephew had left the briefcase on the sidewalk as they were closing for the night. Each thought the other had picked it up. They were nearly home when they discovered the truth. They assumed someone had already taken off with the valuables, and so they decided not to race back to the store.

Shah rewarded David with $30 and Charles with $40.

"It would have been hard to spend the money with my conscience bothering me," David said. "I'd be afraid someone was looking for me."

Don't call me, I'll call you: Todd Towlen of Winchester, Virginia, was 17 when he started getting checks from his late grandfather's insurance policy, in 1977. Monthly, like clockwork, the checks came in the mail: "Pay to the order of Todd W. Towlen—32,000 dollars and no/100 cents."

Todd hadn't expected that much. After the first check arrived, he telephoned the life insurance company. He told them there must be some mistake.

No use. The checks kept coming—"32,000 dollars and no/100 cents"—every month for 2½ years.

Then one bleak day a key-punch operator noticed that a computer was being naughty. It put extra zeros on all Todd's checks. He was supposed to be getting $32 a month.

A vice-president, one of those sticklers for detail, got on the horn. He informed Todd that the insurance company wanted the money returned, less $32 a month.

Not being a grouchy sort, Todd wrote out a check (that included interest) for more than a million dollars.

Talk about bases loaded: In 1980, Thomas Wahlman, 27, a Wall Street clerk, found a valise containing nearly $5 million in stocks belonging to the First Boston Corporation.

Wahlman immediately returned the stocks and daydreamed about the reward. Four weeks later it came—tickets to a New York Mets baseball game.

"I'm not even a baseball fan," Wahlman lamented.

His good deed, however, did not go entirely uncashed. Some fan of honesty read his story in the newspaper and sent him a check for $10.

Far from the maddening crowd: David Gadomski, 13, was on his way to visit a friend in 1979 when his gaze fell upon a blue chest lying in a roadside ditch near his home in Groton, Massachusetts. He went over to have a closer look.

The chest was filled with "all kinds of Harlem Globetrotters stuff": pennants, posters, little basketballs, and a wad of money.

"I flicked through the wad," David said, "and all I could see were fives, tens, and twenties."

He had never seen so much money. He didn't realize there was $1,500 in the wad. He stopped counting at $300 and hurried to tell the police.

The $1,500 was just the beginning. Buried under some

pennants, police uncovered a cardboard box containing $35,000 in cash.

The chest belonged to the Curtis Lentz Corporation, which operated the souvenir business for the Harlem Globetrotters. Thieves had broken into the basketball team's bus and stolen the chest. After removing everything they thought was valuable, they had dumped the chest into the ditch.

David got a letter of praise from his town's police chief and a $500 reward from the Curtis Lentz Corporation.

Yes, he had thought about keeping the money.

"It would have been useful," he admitted. "But if my mother had ever found out that I kept it, she'd have thrown me out of the house."

Cutting it close: Brian Carlson, 17, a busboy in a Chicago, Illinois, restaurant in 1979, cleaned off a table that had more than dirty dishes on it. It had $22,861 stuffed into a small black shaving kit.

A high-school senior, Brian earned $2.40 an hour. When he opened the kit, he saw the chance of "going

where it's warm." After tussling with his conscience, however, he gave the kit to the restaurant manager.

Kit and cash were the property of Joseph T. Faust, 71, of Marathon, Florida. Faust had just buried his wife. He was still in shock when he stopped for a bite on the way to the airport.

Cold cash: Todd Running, 14, dropped a pencil into a floor air-conditioning duct at school one steamy July afternoon in 1981. He reached down for it and came up with a handful of $100 bills.

Heart pounding, he continued to dip his hand into the duct till he had cleaned it of $40,600. Some of the bills were loose. Others were in bundles bound with rubber bands and paper strips.

Todd, of Lake Worth, Florida, was attending a summer math class when the duct yielded its treasures. Finding the money was easy. Keeping it was something else.

The South County Drug Abuse Foundation, which owned the trailer in which the class was held, claimed the money.

The Boynton Beach School Board, which conducted the summer school class, maintained the money belonged to it.

The math teacher, John Montgomery, said the money should go to him. He had removed the rusted-shut vents from the duct before class in order to cool the trailer, thus allowing Todd to find all that cash.

The following July, Judge Carl Harper made losers and weepers out of the drug abuse foundation, the school board, and the teacher. He ruled in favor of Todd.

"He found it and I want him to get it," Judge Harper said. But the judge put the money—$40,600, plus $2,330 in interest—into a bank account controlled by Todd's mother till Todd reached 18. Added the judge: "I'm not going to give him forty thousand dollars to go out and buy bubble gum."

You wonderful you, Wakamatsu: In 1979, Castleton Brian, a British businessman, thought Santa Claus was a taxi driver in Tokyo, Japan.

Brian, 43, stepped from a cab in the city's downtown area late Christmas Eve. He left behind his suitcase loaded with $17,900 in cash.

Arriving home, he realized his blunder and called the police. He had little hope of ever seeing his money again.

On Christmas Day the police called him. They had his suitcase and every cent of the $17,900. The taxi driver, Ryuji Wakamatsu, had found it on the back seat of his cab and had taken it to the police station Christmas morning.

A thousand to one: In 1979, Donald Louk, 30, of Franklin Township, New Jersey, was on his way to business school when he found $415,000 in the street. The money was in two sacks that had fallen out the back door of an armored truck.

Louk, a disabled veteran, feasted his eyes on the cash for a few seconds.

"The first thing I thought about was whether I should turn in the money or run off with it," he said. "But it wasn't mine. My parents raised me to be honest."

He notified the police.

The armored truck company presented him with $1,000 and a job offer. Louk, whose income was a $138 weekly disability check, was disappointed. "That just doesn't balance the book," he said.

The Middlesex County Police Chiefs' Association agreed. The chiefs raised another $1,000 to reward Louk because they wanted "to encourage anyone who finds that kind of money to turn it in."

Do-re-me—no, do-re-u: Bobby Yarbrough opened an envelope from the Internal Revenue Service in 1982 and gasped. Inside was a refund check for $86,407.52.

His dreams ran wild till he called the IRS and learned that every penny was a mistake. Worse, he *owed* $30.

Yarbrough brought the check to the IRS in Jacksonville, Florida. No one thanked him for his honesty. They simply took the check—and his $30.

Sign of the times: A couple living in Cleveland, Ohio, found a wallet containing $65 in cash and a $300 money order outside a supermarket in 1982. They returned it to its owner, but asked the local newspaper not to publish their names.

The wife told the newspaper that she had read of a man who was ridiculed and harassed when he returned a large sum of money he'd found. She and her husband didn't want any publicity.

"You know, it's crazy," she said. "We did something good, and we're almost ashamed of it."

Seek, and ye shall find: In 1929, Ben Jaymin, a New York City businessman, visited his brother's family, who were vacationing on the French Riviera. To amuse his young nieces and nephews, Jaymin searched the suite of hotel rooms for "hidden treasure."

After feeling under all the chair cushions, he stepped into a closet. A 6-footer, he ran his hand along the back of the top shelf. His finger tips brushed a hard object.

"Treasure!" he cried playfully.

The children squealed with delight. They squealed even louder as they watched him take down a richly decorated box. Unbelievably, it was filled with earrings, brooches, rings, bracelets, and necklaces.

Jaymin assumed the jewels were fakes, and he allowed the children to play at being kings and queens. After half an

hour, he went downstairs to the hotel office and reported his find.

The hotel manager was aghast. Six months earlier, he had fired a maid on suspicion of stealing the jewels.

Actually, the jewels had been placed out of sight by a wealthy guest. Forgetting where she had hidden them, she had accused the maid of theft.

Far from being fakes, the jewels were genuine and worth more than $100,000.

An attempt to compensate the maid failed. The unfortunate woman had fled the area in disgrace.

Everything you've always wanted to know about banks: Betty Brown of St. Louis, Missouri, purchased a $35 money order at a bank in 1979. Back home, she discovered the money order had been issued for $1,000,035.

She returned it to the bank and was rewarded with two neckties and a calendar.

Vintage 1957: Curtis Stoldt and his girlfriend, Andrea Golden, were digging for antique bottles in 1981 when they hit pay dirt.

The couple had picked a spot at random in a wooded field in Windsor, Connecticut. After digging just below the surface, Stoldt clinked into a pile of coins. He shoved aside a rock and unearthed a vein of money some 18 inches across and running down nearly 16 inches.

Stoldt thought he'd struck coins that someone had hidden instead of taking to the bank. But when he began poking into greenbacks, he muttered, "This is trouble."

The police finished the digging. The cash, along with check stubs, had been buried in a burlap sack that had rotted away. Only $11,653 of the bills could be counted. The rest were too decomposed.

Some of the check stubs bore the name Hartford Machine Screw Company. That was enough to link the money to a robbery that took place back in 1957. A Hartford Machine Screw Company payroll of $66,573 had been stolen from an armored car and never recovered.

The money was finally awarded to Aetna Life and Casualty, the insurance firm that had paid the $66,573 claim. Aetna gave Stoldt and Golden $1,500 each for their honesty.

The reward, however, could not make up for the loss of

a promising bottle-hunting ground. Treasure seekers had taken over the wooded field in the hope of finding more loot.

"I'm disappointed because there would have been a lot of nice bottles there," Stoldt said. "We had just begun to search."

That's the ticket: In 1979, Earl Sterry, Jr., 16, of Southbury, Connecticut, was hoping to find enough deposit soda bottles in trash cans to buy potato chips. He wound up finding $10,000.

Earl was hunting through some trash when he came across a winning lottery ticket. He recognized the winning combination of two aces and a joker.

He raced home. "Mom," he gasped, "you're not going to believe what happened."

As he was underage, his mother cashed in the $10,000 ticket for him.

I been walkin' on the railroad: Eric DeWild, 15, was walking along the railroad tracks trying to make a decision. It was 2 A.M., March 16, 1983, and he was having second thoughts.

The slight, sandy-haired orphan was running away from home. The day before, he had played hooky from school. Modena Trost, an aunt with whom he lived in Hollywood, Florida, had found out.

Although ashamed and resentful, Eric struggled with his thoughts. The farther he walked, the more his resentment cooled, the more he realized he was making a mistake.

Reaching the point where Hollywood's Taft Street meets the Seacoast Railroad, he saw a yellow bank bag and a blue jewelry box lying on the gravel. Inside them were coins, watches, brooches, necklaces, and several unmounted stones wrapped in tissue. Then and there, Eric gave up the idea of running away.

Several hours later he was at McNicol Junior High School showing off his find. He let some of his teachers and classmates try on the jewelry. He gave a man's ring and a few necklaces to friends. Everyone, especially Eric, believed he had found inexpensive costume jewelry.

Still, he had begun to wonder and to daydream. Could

the jewels be real? To learn the truth, he took them to a jeweler. When the man offered to buy the entire lot right off, Eric realized what he had found, and said no thanks. He went home and dumped the treasure on the living room couch.

His aunt sensed its value immediately, and she knew what to do. "Eric, we have to turn this over to the police."

After a bath and a glass of milk, Eric was moved to agree with her. The next day he got back the gifts he had given friends and went to the police station.

As he laid out the treasures one by one on a desk, an officer looked at him and joked, "What are you doing here? Why aren't you at the airport waiting for a plane to Brazil?"

Jokes aside, the police frowned upon Eric's story. The collection consisted of both brand-new merchandise and antiques; it wasn't what one person would probably own. Eric was suspected of pulling off a series of burglaries. "You're in deep trouble," he was told.

In order to prove his innocence, Eric took detectives to the spot on the railroad tracks. Many more pieces were still lying around loose.

The police presumed the items had been stolen. State-wide bulletins were sent out to locate the true owners. Claims came in from all over the United States, Mexico, Canada, and England. The police spent 2,000 hours and $30,000 to investigate 1,400 claims. None checked out.

After the 6-month waiting period required by Florida law, the treasure was returned to Eric. It belonged to him.

The wait had been far from easy for Eric and his aunt. Reporters and camera crews staked out their run-down frame house. The rags-to-riches tale brought hundreds of telephone calls, including threatening ones. His aunt had to change her telephone number. Eric had to go into hiding for days.

A strange man had been seen in their driveway shortly after Eric had found the jewels. Then a hit-and-run driver had knocked Eric off his moped.

Eric and his aunt, who had raised him since his mother's death when he was seven, began to wonder if the jewels were worth it all.

On June 12, 1984, they may have changed their minds. They sat with their attorney, Charles O. Morgan, at Christie's, a respected auction house in New York City. Bidding on the jewels began. A man's 5.9-carat ring went for $27,000. Another ring brought $19,000. The day ended with Eric richer by $281,490.

On June 21, an auction of lesser pieces, some of them partly crushed by train wheels, added $63,307, a total of $344,797 for the 116 pieces sold.

Eric returned to Florida, planning to buy his aunt a "dream house" and a car for himself. He also wanted to make a donation to the Christian Broadcasting Network. Attorney Morgan said the rest of the money would be put in a trust fund.

Reading, Writing, and . . . Really?

Sleeping smart: Tests indicate that the best time to learn is at night before going to bed. And the shorter the period

I'M READY FOR BED, DAD.

between study and bedtime, the more likely you are to retain new knowledge.

That's lice: Students in Stuttgart, West Germany, bought head lice for about $2.60 each in 1981. They used the lice as an excuse to be barred from class.

Wernher von Braun, the foremost German rocket scientist in World War II, failed both math and physics in high school.

Lights shout: Traffic lights were set up in a cafeteria of the Ellendale Elementary School in Memphis, Tennessee, in 1982.

As long as the noise level stayed below a roar, the green light shone. Once the noise climbed to 72 decibels on a sound meter, the yellow came on.

If the noise didn't drop, the light turned to red. All the talk had to cease or talkers were sent to the principal's office.

Robert Kennedy, the U.S. Attorney General during the presidency of his brother, John F. Kennedy, flunked third grade.

Seeing red: In 1957, Will Judy, a Chicago, Illinois, publisher, willed to Juanita College of Pennsylvania funds for a dormitory room in honor of his redheaded wife. There was one condition: the room had to be occupied by redheaded students.

Watt a mind: Thomas Alva Edison invented the electric light bulb and held more than 1,000 patents, but was not a good student.

"I remember," he said, "that I was never able to get along at school. I was always at the foot of the class."

His teachers considered him "addled." His father thought him "stupid."

The United States Office of Education paid Boston University $219,592 to teach college students how to watch television.

More than half of the 535 first-year teachers in the Dallas (Texas) School District (the eighth largest district in the country) flunked a mental aptitude test in 1979. The test was normally given to 13-year-olds.

Jerry Parsons, principal of an elementary school in Salida, Colorado, wanted to hold a spelling bee in 1982 and asked his teachers for some words. He got them—and a shock. The teachers' list included feeble, spelled *feable*; formerly, spelled *formorly*; and bookkeeping, spelled *bookeeping*.

In 1965, Benjamin Bloom of the University of Chicago announced findings on human intelligence that have slowly gained acceptance over the years.

According to Bloom, half of human intelligence is set by age 4. An additional 30 percent is reached by age 8. And 33

percent of whatever school skills children have by 18 is developed before age 6.

It's all relative: Albert Einstein, one of the most creative scientific minds in history, did not speak until he was 6. His family believed him slow-witted.

It is said that his father once asked Albert's headmaster what profession his son should follow. The answer was simply: "It doesn't matter. He'll never make a success of anything."

And bring your teeth: Alldora Bjarnadottir of Iceland wondered why she was bombarded with literature preparing her for elementary school. Being 107, she thought she was too old to start classes all over again.

In 1980 officials pinpointed the goof. Every citizen of Iceland must go to school by age 7. A government computer, which couldn't count past 100, kicked out her name as a 7-year-old.

Winston Churchill, Great Britain's prime minister during World War II, was a poor student. At his school, Harrow, he remained in the lowest form 3 times as long as anyone else and was a failure at Latin and Greek.

Benjamin Franklin attended school for only 2 years—from age 8 to age 10.

Paddle-cake, paddle-cake: The Meadowview Middle School in Morristown, Tennessee, was burglarized in 1980. Only 10 articles were stolen. The loot: 10 wooden paddles, 1 from each teacher's desk.

Hans Christian Andersen, whose stories are read throughout the world, was considered a backward child.

In 1822, Andersen was admitted to the grammar school in Slagelse, Denmark. Four years later his headmaster, Simon Søresen Meisling, mentioned Andersen in a letter to a friend: Andersen, wrote Meisling, was "in want of the most necessary preliminary knowledge. In spite of his advanced age, he was put in the lowest class but one." Andersen was then 17.

When he left school, Andersen was told by Meisling that his writings would "rot as waste paper," and that he would end up in a lunatic asylum.

Eleven years afterward, Andersen met Meisling, shabby and out of work, on the streets of Copenhagen. "Oh, how it touched me," wrote Andersen, "to hear him admit, 'Honor is yours, shame is mine.'"

If you want to become a cowboy, have a look at tiny Sul Ross State University in Alpin, Texas.

You can learn to shoe your own horse, judge cows, breed dogs, feed goats, and "break" a bucking bronco.

Yes, there's a football team. The scholarships, however, go to the rodeo riders.

The nation's longest-overdue book was borrowed in 1823 from the University of Cincinnati Medical Library. A work on febrile diseases, it was returned on December 7, 1968, by the borrower's great-grandson Richard Dogg.

He was not asked to pay the fine—$2,264.

It's smart to be early: Studies of more than 6,000 boys and girls, 12 to 18, revealed that boys who reached puberty early scored better on standard intelligence and achievement tests than did late developers.

The difference was not found among girls. But a surprising fact did show up. Girls who developed late equaled or outdid boys in mathematics. Usually, adolescent girls fall behind boys in mathematical ability, and the early-maturing girls who were studied did just that.

First-born kids are usually the smartest, though they don't have as many friends as other kids. Last-born kids are commonly the most popular on the playground.

Ride 'em, schoolgirl: Kyle MacKay, 18, galloped off to college in 1981. Astride her Morgan, Dunrovin Jay, she rode from her home in Richfield Springs, New York, to Carleton College in Minnesota.

"Ever since I was seven years old, I've dreamed of riding a horse across country," she said. "I've always wanted to be able to ride as long as I want and as far as I want."

General George S. Patton, possibly the best combat leader in World War II, suffered from dyslexia and could not read at the age of 12. It took him an extra year to get through West Point.

Jay Luo, son of immigrants from Taiwan, became the youngest college graduate in United States history when he was graduated from Boise State (Idaho) University in 1982 with a degree in mathematics. He was 12.

Guilty: Only 36 of the 78 men and women who in 1981 took the test to become lawyers in Vermont passed it. For once, don't blame the students. One examiner didn't understand the grading system. He gave the lowest marks for the best answers and the highest marks for the worst.

Louisa May Alcott, author of *Little Women*, sent an early manuscript to a publisher and received it back with the advice, "Stick to your teaching, Miss Alcott. You will never be a writer."

According to Doyle: Mail is still being sent to Sherlock Holmes almost a century after the greatest detective in British fiction appeared in the first of 60 stories by Sir Arthur Conan Doyle.

The letters seek advice or report the sighting of dangerous criminals or describe missing goods. They are addressed to Holmes at his storybook lodgings, 221-B Baker

Street, and reach the building occupied by the Abbey National Building Society, a savings and loan association, at 215–230 Baker Street. Each letter is answered, said an association spokesman, "because it is a very English thing to do."

Giuseppe Verdi, the great composer of operas, was refused a scholarship to a music conservatory in Milan, Italy, because he lacked talent. After he had gained international fame, the conservatory was renamed the Verdi Conservatory of Music.

Aspirin Alley

Americans suffer from a personality cult. We look up to men and women who often are no more than wealthy, good-looking, or showoffs.

Meantime, the underdog, the innocent victim, the honest blunderer, and the harmless klutz are ignored. To correct this historic injustice, Aspirin Alley welcomes:

—Timothy George, 18, a part-time busboy at a restaurant in Vallejo, California, who in 1982 chased and captured a mugger who had robbed a customer in the men's room.

Timothy was promptly fired for "leaving work and fighting."

—The young man in Taiwan who wrote 700 love letters to his girlfriend in the years 1974–76 trying to woo her into marriage. He succeeded. She married the postman who delivered the letters.

—Alan Broadhurst, 36, a painter, of Barnsley, England, who forgot to mail his wife's all-correct coupon to a British football pool in 1981. It would have been worth £750,000—about $1.75 million.

—The Philadelphia, Pennsylvania, city fathers, who in 1976 discovered that the statue of Guglielmo Marconi in Marconi Plaza was really of Christopher Columbus.

—Peter Minuit, the Dutchman, who in 1626 became the first victim of American real estate agents. He purchased Manhattan Island for $24 in beads, needles, buttons, and fabrics from the fast-talking Canarsee Indians, who forthwith took off for parts unknown.

Eventually, the Dutch had to buy Manhattan Island from the real owners, the Weckquaresgeeks.

—Ruth Clarke, 23, of London, England, who underwent surgery to correct a lifelong breathing problem in 1981. She was presented with a tiddlywink, which doctors had removed from her nose.

Clarke vaguely recalled losing the disk as a tot, but she didn't dream it was right under her nose all the time.

—Jackie Johnson, 11, who landed a largemouth bass while fishing with his father from the bank of a Florida lake in 1981. The bass weighed nearly 23 pounds on a pocket scale.

Jackie later learned that a largemouth bass that topped the 22-pound-4-ounce record bass caught in 1932 was worth a small fortune to the lucky angler.

By then it was too late. Jackie's bass couldn't be officially weighed. It had been eaten.

—Alan Lewis, 35, a bus driver in Monmouth, Wales, who in 1982 drove his double-decker bus under the arch of a thirteenth-century bridge gatehouse and sheared off half the upper deck.

"I usually drive single-deckers," he explained. "I just forgot I was in a double-decker."

Shear forgetfulness.

—The loyal party members who gave Philadelphia Congressman William Barrett 75 percent of the votes in the 1976 Democratic primary without inquiring into his whereabouts.

Barrett had been dead for 2 weeks.

—The skyjacker who in 1976 grabbed an airline attendant, ordered her to have the plane flown to Detroit, and was told, "That's where we're going."

—The 300 typists who didn't worry about rushing home to their children when they competed in the regional type-off for the World's Fastest Typist Contest in 1982. They lost to Brenda Cooper, a housewife from South Plainfield, New Jersey. She worried "that I wouldn't finish fast enough to be there when Melanie got home from school."

—The Vancouver, Washington, youth who in 1982 tried to beat his curfew by sneaking down the chimney at 3 A.M. He had to be freed by firemen.

Not only did a false flue keep him from emerging through the fireplace, but the chimney belonged to the house next door to his.

—The hotel cashier in Bangkok, Thailand, who was convicted of embezzling $12,000 in 1981. Because he cooperated with the court, his sentence was reduced—from 865 years to 576 years.

—The city council of Worland, Wyoming, which in 1972 made it illegal for drivers on city streets to be wildly happy while stepping on the gas. The law was meant to keep drivers from undue "acceleration." But the word printed was "exhilaration." Ten years went by before the error was corrected.

You still can't speed through Worland, but you don't have to look so glum anymore.

—The heavyset man who in 1982 lumbered into a pawnshop in Houston, Texas, and tried unsuccessfully to cash a $789 check that was made out to Earnestine and Robert Hayes. He claimed that his mother had expected twins, and when only he was born, she gave him both names.

—Peter Stankiewicz of Rockville, Maryland, who stopped his car in 1981 and dived into the Potomac River to rescue a driver whose lumber truck had crashed through a bridge railing and plunged 60 feet into the icy water. After hauling the driver to shore, Stankiewicz was informed that his car had been towed to the pound because it was blocking traffic.

—Edward Misrapov, 20, of Moscow, Russia, who in 1981 burglarized an apartment, but couldn't resist lingering to play the piano. Neighbors complained of the noise, and the cops waltzed in and arrested him.

—Brian Sanderson, 43, of Staffordshire, England, who in 1981 shut the front door of his home and watched three-fourths of the two-story, 120-year-old house collapse around him in a pile of dust and rubble. Miraculously,

Sanderson, his wife, and their two children were not seriously hurt.

—Jennie Seff of London, England, who in 1981 was testing the batteries in her bright red robot, Robotham, when it suddenly went out of control.

"He seemed to have a mind of his own," panted Seff.

Robotham, a 4-foot, 49-pounder that can walk and shake hands, chased her across the office.

—George Wittmeier of Kirland, Washington, who was notified in 1981 by the Internal Revenue Service that he underpaid his federal income tax by a penny and therefore would be fined $159.78.

—The inmates at the prison in Concord, New Hampshire, who make the state's license plates, which bear the motto LIVE FREE OR DIE.

—Bryon W. Frierson, vice-president of a land development company, who tried to show a buyer a five-room house in Sugar Land, Texas, in 1980, but couldn't. The house had been swiped from its foundations.

Frierson offered a $200 reward to anyone who noticed the sudden appearance in his neighborhood of a new white house with green trim and an asbestos roof.

—Betty Tudor, 50, of London, England, who decided to buy a moped in 1981 after flunking 7 driver's tests, spending money on 273 driving lessons, and being banned by 3 driving schools.

Tudor also wore out 9 driving instructors. "One of them ended up in a mental hospital," she said. "But I'm not certain I was totally to blame."

—All the folks who moved to Gainesville, Florida, after reading a 1980 FBI report that the city was among the safest places to live in the U.S. When the printing error was corrected, Gainesville made the Top 10 in crimes, ranking fourth behind Miami, Atlantic City, and Las Vegas.

—Atari, Inc., maker of video games, which in 1981 sponsored the world championship of its Asteroids game, won by free-spoken Andy Breyer, 15, of Chicago, Illinois.

Andy took home $5,000, and his frankness stiffened company representatives. "I don't like Asteroids that much," was Andy's opening comment. Well, now . . . did he find another Atari game, Space Invaders, more to his liking? "It's kind of boring," was the reply. How much money had he spent playing video games? "Oh, about fifty cents at most," Andy said. "I don't like to waste my money on this stuff."

The Atari officials disappeared into the crowd.

—Matt Brooks of Cheshire, England, a furnaceman, who thought he was 63 years old in 1981. When he applied for early retirement, he learned that he was really 79 and should have retired 14 years earlier.

—Ray Wright of Philadelphia, Pennsylvania, who in 1978 left flyers on autos that read: "If you didn't see me put this on your windshield, I could have just as easily stolen your car." While he was thusly promoting his burglar alarm business, someone stole his truck.

—David Jacarusso, 30, who in 1981 parachuted from a plane over New York City intending to land on one of the World Trade Center towers—and came down in a pile of garbage in Battery Park.

—The Joseph A. Bank Clothiers, Inc., of Atlanta, Georgia, which requested that the word "Inc." be dropped from its listing in the 1982 telephone directory yellow pages. As a result, the store was listed as "Drop Inc."

—Mr. and Mrs. M. Lewenetz, who stepped off a plane from Russia in 1981 thinking they were in sunny St. Petersburg, Florida. Instead they were in the tiny town of Petersburg, Alaska. An airport official in Moscow had left off the "St." when he filled out their tickets.

—The Chevrolet division of General Motors, which tried unsuccessfully to sell its Nova automobiles in Latin America. In Spanish, Nova, spelled as two words, *no va*, but pronounced the same, means "does not go."

—Cross-country skier Randy Winowieki of Glenn Haven, Michigan, who didn't hear the avalanche that buried him for 3½ hours in 1982. He was listening to music on stereo headphones.

—Gerald Steindam, 24, of Miami, Florida, who had vowed never to fly Eastern Airlines' flight 401 (New York–Miami) after luckily missing a flight 401 in 1972 that went down in the Everglades.

In 1980 he overcame his superstitious fear and took the flight. The plane was hijacked to Cuba.

—The Canadian town of New Dundee, which changed its name to Dire Straits after Prime Minister Pierre Elliot Trudeau announced in 1981 that budget cutbacks meant halting aid to all towns except those "in dire straits."

—The 20-year-old Indian woman whom game wardens arrested in 1978 for killing a tiger with an ax when it approached her as she gathered wood. Slaying tigers is unlawful in India.

—Gerald Franz, 56, who set out to prove that "kite power" really works. In 1982 he departed from Cape Cod, Massachusetts, for England in a 16-foot kayak pulled by 5

nylon kites. The winds kept blowing him back to shore. After an hour he said the heck with it.

—Ralph J. Perk, mayor of Cleveland, who in 1972 manned a welding torch at the opening ceremonies for a new office building and set his hair on fire.

—New York City, which spent $54,000 in 1981 for an exhibit to lure foreign manufacturers to the city. The display, titled "Make It in New York," was made in New Jersey.

—The surgeons who arrived in Los Angeles, California, to perform a kidney transplant operation in 1980 and left the kidney at the airport. It was retrieved in time.

—Lois Stratton, who, campaigning for reelection as a state representative in Washington in 1982, made a speech to the wrong audience. She addressed the American Association of Retired Persons. Down the hall the Retired Public Employees Organization wondered where their luncheon speaker was.

At least she was close.

—Edward Stainer of Blaydon, England, who searched for the source of a draft in his living room for 20 years. In

1971 he pulled up a floorboard—and stared into a hole 1,000 feet deep.

—The New York City Personnel Department, which in 1982 removed sexism from nearly all job titles. One nose-catching change was from "seamstress" to "sewer," pronounced *sower*, and not to be confused with certain underground works of the same spelling.

—John Batt, who was out of the country and so missed by 3 days the 1-year deadline for claiming his $50,000 winnings in the New Jersey State Lottery.

—The doctors in Los Angeles, California, who went on strike in 1976 to protest the soaring cost of malpractice insurance. During the strike, the death rate in the area dropped 18 percent.

—The Department of Agriculture, which considered saving money in its school-lunch program in 1981 by classifying ketchup and pickle relish as vegetables and sunflower seeds as meat.

—Joseph P. Stevens, 51, of Fall River, Massachusetts, who spotted his stolen car going by him on a Connecticut highway in 1980. He recognized the 1971 sedan by the rag hanging from the smashed trunk and the insurance company sticker on the bumper. The car, riding the back of a flatbed trailer, had been crushed into junk metal 18 feet long and 6 inches high.

—The Fairfax County (Virginia) firemen who in 1977 discovered that their helmets had an annoying habit of melting in the heat.

—Keith McGuigan of Oshawa, Canada, who drove to an auto wrecker in 1981 in search of a door latch for his 1972 Rambler. An hour later he found the latch, but not his car. He had parked it in a row of junkers waiting to be crushed, and his Rambler had become a sub-subcompact.

—The five elderly citizens of Spokane, Washington, who in 1981 had cause to wail but not the means to gnash. After having their teeth removed because the state paid the bill, they were informed that owing to budget cuts there was no money for false teeth.

ABOUT THE AUTHOR

DONALD J. SOBOL is the author of the highly acclaimed Encyclopedia Brown books. His awards for these books include the Pacific Northwest Reader's Choice Award for *Encyclopedia Brown Keeps the Peace* and a special Edgar from the Mystery Writers of America for his contribution to mystery writing in the United States.

Donald Sobol is married and has three children. A native of New York, he now lives in Florida.

ABOUT THE ILLUSTRATOR

SAL MURDOCCA is the illustrator of many popular books for young readers, including *Cats to Count* and *Tom the TV Cat*. As both author and illustrator he has written *The Nothings* and the critically acclaimed *The Hero of Hamblett* and *Sir Hamm and the Golden Sundial*. Sal Murdocca lives in Rockland County, New York, with his daughter and two cats. In his spare time he plays tennis and rides his racing bicycle.